anythink

D0605580

RAPTORS!
BUZZARDS

Henry Abbot

PowerKiDS press.

New York

Published in 2016 by The Rosen Publishing Group, Inc.
29 East 21st Street, New York, NY 10010

First Edition

Editor: Sarah Machajewski
Book Design: Mickey Harmon

Photo Credits: Cover series logo Elena Paletskaya/Shutterstock.com; cover, pp. 1, 3, 4, 6, 8, 10, 12, 14, 16, 18, 20, 22–24 (top and bottom texture, raptor factor box) Picsfive/Shutterstock.com; cover (background scene) M. Pellinni/Shutterstock.com; cover, p. 22 (buzzard perched) Piotr Krzeslak/Shutterstock.com; cover (buzzard flying), p. 13 Adam Fichna/Shutterstock.com; p. 5 Chris Humphries/Shutterstock.com; p. 7 (main) Neil Burton/Shutterstock.com; p. 7 (inset) Tomasz Czadowski/Shutterstock.com; p. 8 phdwhite/Shutterstock.com; p. 9 davemhuntphotography/Shutterstock.com; p. 11 Mike Powles/Oxford Scientific/Getty Images; p. 15 rorue/Shutterstock.com; p. 17 Kristian Bell/Moment/Getty Images; p. 18 Frank Greenaway/Dorling Kindersley/Getty Images; p. 19 alarifoto/Vetta/Getty Images; p. 21 Vishnevskiy Vasily/Shutterstock.com.

Library of Congress Cataloging-in-Publication Data

Abbott, Henry, author.
 Buzzards / Henry Abbott.
     pages cm. — (Raptors!)
  Includes index.
ISBN 978-1-5081-4236-2 (pbk.)
ISBN 978-1-5081-4237-9 (6 pack)
ISBN 978-1-5081-4238-6 (library binding)
1. Buzzards—Juvenile literature. 2. Vultures—Juvenile literature. 3. Birds of prey—Juvenile literature. I. Title.
QL696.F3A23 2016
598.9—dc23
                                        2015023449

Manufactured in the United States of America

CPSIA Compliance Information: Batch #BW16PK: For Further Information contact Rosen Publishing, New York, New York at 1-800-237-9932

Contents

Look to the Sky

  Near the wooded areas of Europe, it's common to see a medium-sized bird slowly circling the sky. People often see these birds diving from a tree branch to catch **prey**. When people see these things happen, it's likely they've seen a European buzzard.

  Buzzards are a kind of bird in the raptor family. Buzzards have many features that make them **unique**. Read on to learn more about these birds and the special family of raptors they belong to.

> This buzzard keeps an eye out for its next meal as it flies through the sky.

5

What Makes a Bird a Raptor?

Before you can learn about buzzards, you must learn about raptors. Like all birds, raptors have wings and feathers, and they lay eggs. However, a bird must have four other features in order to be called a raptor.

All raptors have hooked beaks. This is a major difference between raptors and other birds. Raptors also have feet with sharp talons, or claws, and very good eyesight. Finally, raptors are carnivores. A carnivore is an animal that only eats meat.

RAPTOR FACTOR

Raptors are also called birds of prey.

hooked beak

sharp talons

good eyesight

The raptor family includes buzzards, hawks, eagles, falcons, vultures, and owls.

What's in a Name?

There are about 30 species, or kinds, of buzzards. Buzzards belong to an animal group named *Buteo*. In Europe, the name "buzzard" is used to talk about birds that are part of the *Buteo* group. In fact, the common buzzard's scientific name is *Buteo buteo*.

In the Americas, the name "buzzard" is used to talk about vultures, which are another kind of raptor. This book focuses on the buzzards found in Europe.

honey buzzard

common buzzard

Honey buzzards and common buzzards are two species in the buzzard family. Although they're different species, they're similar in how they look and act.

Buzzards in the Wild

Buzzards live all across Europe, except in very hot and very cold places. The common buzzard is one of the most familiar species. Its **habitat** ranges from northern Europe to the areas around the Mediterranean Sea. The honey buzzard is another familiar species.

No matter where buzzards live, their habitats are often similar. They live in hilly, wooded areas. They can live near farmlands and forests, too. These are places that have plenty of food for buzzards to hunt.

RAPTOR FACTOR

In the United Kingdom, buzzards are sometimes spotted in towns and cities.

Woods, forests, and farmlands are home to many of the animals buzzards like to eat.

Buzzard Body

How can you tell a buzzard apart from other raptors? Look at its body when it's flying. A buzzard has broad wings and a large, rounded tail. Other raptors don't have these kinds of wings and tails.

You may also be able to **identify** a buzzard by its colors. Most buzzards' wings are dark brown at the top and light brown or white at the bottom. The underside is often striped. However, even birds of the same species can have very different colors.

RAPTOR FACTOR

Wingspan is the measurement from the tip of one wing to the tip of the other.

A buzzard's wingspan is usually between 43 and 54 inches (109 and 137 cm).

Buzzard Behavior

If birds are known for anything, it's flying. However, when it comes to buzzards, it might be better to say they **soar**. They beat their wings slowly and ride on wind currents. This helps them **glide** in the air, which gives them a better chance at seeing prey on the ground.

When buzzards aren't flying, they may be perching. Perching is when a bird rests on something. Perching on high branches or buildings allows buzzards to look down and spot prey.

Buzzards have excellent eyesight, which is how they see tiny prey when they're high in the sky.

Bird of Prey

Buzzards are birds of prey, so they must hunt their food. They eat small rodents, which are animals such as mice, squirrels, and rats. These animals are light enough for a buzzard to carry in its claws. They also eat frogs, bugs, and worms.

Buzzards have three main ways of hunting. They see prey from their perch and swoop down to grab it. They fly over open land and then dive at prey when they see it. Or they walk on the ground and look for food.

RAPTOR FACTOR

Buzzards also eat carrion, which is a word for dead animals.

A buzzard uses its strong claws to carry its prey to its feeding spot. Then, it uses its sharp beak to tear apart the animal's flesh.

Building a Home

Like most bird species, buzzards build nests. Nests are built in trees, on cliffs, or in another high location that's out of the way. Both male and female birds help build the nest. They use branches and twigs to build it. Then, they line it with soft plants such as grass.

Common buzzards have between one and three nesting places. They can use a different nest each year or reuse an old one. Nests are about 3.3 feet (1 m) wide and 24 inches (61 cm) deep.

This is a top-down view of a common buzzard's nest.

Buzzards are very **territorial**. If another bird tries to come near their nesting place, they will attack it.

Buzzard Babies

Once a nest is built, it's time for a buzzard to lay eggs. Females lay between two and four eggs at a time. Buzzard eggs are white with brown or red spots. The group of eggs is called a clutch.

Female buzzards sit on the eggs for about 30 days. Then the baby buzzards hatch, or break out of their shell. The male buzzard brings food to the nest for the babies to eat. After about two weeks, the female helps hunt for food.

Baby buzzards leave the nest after about two months. In that time, their parents teach them how to hunt.

Buzzards and People

Buzzards are wild birds. Unfortunately, human activity can have a bad effect on them. When we build in their habitats or cut down trees, buzzards lose places to live. They also lose food, since the animals they eat lose their home, too. Some studies show that 75 **percent** of young buzzards die because they don't have enough food. However, if buzzards survive, they can live up to 25 years! If we leave buzzards and their habitats alone, they'll survive for years to come.

Glossary

glide: To move with a smooth motion, often with little noise.

habitat: The natural home of a person or animal.

identify: To recognize.

percent: A part of a whole, given in terms of parts out of 100.

prey: An animal that is hunted by other animals for food.

soar: To fly or rise high into the air.

territorial: Having to do with an animal defending or protecting its land or home.

unique: Special or different.

23

Index

Websites

Due to the changing nature of Internet links, PowerKids Press has developed an online list of websites related to the subject of this book. This site is updated regularly. Please use this link to access the list: www.powerkidslinks.com/rapt/buzz